DON SMITH

THE SOCIAL MEDIA DILEMMA

*How Social Media is Hijacking Our Minds and What
We Can Do About It*

This book is dedicated to all those who have been affected by the social media dilemma. To those who have had their personal data compromised, their mental health impacted, and their lives consumed by the addictive nature of social media. It is also dedicated to the activists and organizations working tirelessly to bring attention to these issues and create change.

"The social dilemma is not just about social media; it's about our society, our values, and the future we want to create. We have the power to shape that future through our choices and actions."

- TRISTAN HARRIS

Contents

Foreword

In today's fast-paced world, social media has become an integral part of our lives. We use it to connect with friends and family, stay updated on news and current events, and share our thoughts and experiences with others. However, with the increasing use of social media comes a range of challenges and issues that we must grapple with.

The Social Media Dilemma is a comprehensive guide to understanding the impact of social media on our lives and society as a whole. It explores the ways in which social media can be both a force for good and a source of harm, and provides practical tips and strategies for navigating the complex landscape of social media use.

The authors of this book have a wealth of knowledge and experience in the fields of technology, psychology, and social science. They provide a nuanced and insightful analysis of the various issues and challenges associated with social media use, including data privacy, misinformation, and the impact of social media on mental health and well-being.

Through the course of this book, readers will gain a deeper understanding of the role that social media plays in our lives, and the ways in which we can use it more responsibly and effectively. Whether you are a casual social media user or a seasoned professional, this book has something to offer.

I highly recommend The Social Media Dilemma to anyone

who is interested in understanding the impact of social media on our society, and in taking practical steps to promote positive change. This is a timely and important book that provides valuable insights and strategies for navigating the complex landscape of social media use.

Sincerely,

Lyn K. Parrish

Preface

Social media has changed the world in many ways, providing unprecedented opportunities for communication, connection, and community-building. However, with these benefits come significant challenges, including the spread of misinformation, invasion of privacy, and the impact on mental health and well-being. The Social Media Dilemma aims to explore these issues and provide readers with a comprehensive understanding of the role of social media in our lives, the dangers associated with its use, and the strategies we can employ to minimize these risks and promote positive change.

In this book, we bring together experts from various fields to provide a multifaceted view of the social media landscape. We examine the ways in which social media has transformed communication and information dissemination, the psychological and social impacts of excessive social media use, and the ethical considerations associated with data collection and monetization.

The book provides a comprehensive look at the risks and dangers of social media, including the spread of misinformation and the manipulation of public opinion. We also explore the responsibility of social media companies in addressing these issues and discuss the strategies that readers can employ to take control of their social media use and promote positive change.

While social media presents significant challenges, it also

provides us with unique opportunities for positive social change. We examine the ways in which advocacy and social change movements have utilized social media to raise awareness and mobilize support, and we provide readers with tools and strategies for leveraging social media for social good.

Ultimately, The Social Media Dilemma seeks to empower readers to take control of their social media use and promote positive change in their communities and the world. We hope that this book will provide readers with the knowledge and resources they need to navigate the complex world of social **media** and to use these platforms for good.

Acknowledgement

We would like to express our sincere gratitude to all those who have contributed to the creation and publication of this book.

First and foremost, we would like to thank the contributors who shared their expertise and insights on the complex topic of the social media dilemma. Their contributions have enriched this book and deepened our understanding of the issues at hand.

We are also grateful to the publishers and editorial team who have supported us throughout the entire process, from the initial concept development to the final publication. Their dedication and hard work have been invaluable in bringing this book to life.

We extend our thanks to our families and loved ones for their unwavering support and encouragement throughout this journey. They have been our source of inspiration and motivation, and we could not have done this without them.

We also express our appreciation to the many individuals and organizations who are working tirelessly to address the social media dilemma and promote positive change. Their efforts are making a difference, and we hope that this book can contribute to their important work.

Finally, we thank our readers for their interest in this book and their willingness to engage with the important issues it raises. We hope that this book can inspire reflection, conversation, and action, and that together we can create a healthier and more responsible relationship with social media.

Chapter 1: Introduction

Social media has become an integral part of our daily lives, from sharing pictures of our meals to connecting with friends and family around the world. However, with the rise of social media platforms, we are facing a new challenge - the social media dilemma. The social media dilemma refers to the negative impact that social media can have on our mental health, social relationships, and society as a whole.

Social media was initially created to bring people together, provide a platform for communication, and democratize information sharing. It has revolutionized the way we connect with one another, breaking down physical barriers and bringing us closer together. With the advent of social media, people can now connect with others in different parts of the world and share their thoughts and experiences with a global audience.

However, as social media platforms have become more sophisticated and pervasive, they have also started to impact our lives in negative ways. Social media companies have developed algorithms that can track our behavior and tailor our online experiences to keep us engaged for longer periods. This has resulted in an increase in social media addiction, cyberbullying, and social isolation.

The persuasive techniques used by social media platforms have also been a cause for concern. Social media companies use algorithms to create echo chambers that reinforce our beliefs and values, without exposing us to diverse perspectives. This has contributed to the spread of misinformation and fake news, and the erosion of trust in traditional news sources.

The impact of social media is not limited to individuals. Social media has become a powerful tool for shaping public opinion, influencing elections, and driving social movements. Its impact on politics and social change has been significant, with social media often being credited with playing a pivotal role in many recent social and political movements around the world.

In this book, "The Social Dilemma: How Social Media is Hijacking Our Minds and What We Can Do About It," we explore the complex issues surrounding social media and its impact on our lives. We examine the persuasive techniques used by social media platforms, the impact of social media on mental health, the role of social media in shaping societal norms, and the dangers of data collection and misuse.

The purpose of this book is not to demonize social media or suggest that we should abandon it altogether. Rather, we aim to educate readers on the risks and challenges of social media and provide practical strategies for reducing its negative impact. We believe that with awareness and responsible use, social media can continue to be a valuable tool for communication and connection.

Throughout the book, we will provide insights and analysis from experts in psychology, sociology, and technology. We will also share real-life stories and examples to illustrate the impact of social media on individuals and society.

As you read this book, we encourage you to reflect on your

own social media use and consider the steps you can take to create a healthier relationship with social media. Together, we can navigate the social media dilemma and use these platforms to connect, learn, and grow.

Explanation of the social media dilemma

The social media dilemma refers to the negative impact that social media can have on our mental health, social relationships, and society as a whole. Social media platforms have become an integral part of our daily lives, but they can also be addictive, manipulative, and harmful.

One of the main concerns with social media is the persuasive techniques used by these platforms to keep users engaged. Social media companies use algorithms to track user behavior and tailor the user experience to keep users on the platform for longer periods. This can lead to social media addiction, where individuals spend excessive amounts of time on social media, impacting their productivity, mental health, and overall well-being.

Another issue with social media is the impact it can have on mental health. Studies have shown that excessive use of social media can contribute to feelings of anxiety, depression, and loneliness. Social media can create unrealistic expectations and comparisons, leading to negative self-image and self-esteem. Cyberbullying, trolling, and harassment are also common on social media platforms, leading to emotional distress and psychological harm.

Social media can also have a significant impact on social relationships. While social media has made it easier to connect with others, it can also lead to social isolation and loneliness. Social media can create a false sense of connection, where individuals feel like they are connected to others, but in reality, they are only connected through a screen. This can lead to a lack of meaningful human interaction and a deterioration of in-person social relationships.

Finally, social media can have a significant impact on society as a whole. Social media can be used as a tool for spreading misinformation, propaganda, and fake news, impacting public opinion and the democratic process. Social media can also be used to amplify hate speech, incite violence, and promote extremist ideologies, leading to social unrest and division.

In summary, the social media dilemma refers to the complex challenges and risks associated with the use of social media. While social media has brought many benefits, it has also contributed to social, psychological, and societal problems. It is essential to be aware of the social media dilemma and take proactive steps to reduce its negative impact on our lives.

Here are some additional elements that can be added to the explanation of the social media dilemma:

1. Privacy Concerns: Social media platforms collect vast amounts of user data, including personal information, search history, and online behavior. This data can be used for targeted advertising and even sold to third parties. Many users are unaware of how their data is being used, leading to concerns about privacy and data security.

2. Filter Bubbles: Social media algorithms are designed to show users content that is most relevant to them, based on their past behavior and preferences. This can lead to

the creation of filter bubbles, where users only see content that reinforces their existing beliefs and opinions. This can lead to a lack of exposure to diverse viewpoints and a narrowing of the user's worldview.

3. Comparison Culture: Social media can create a culture of comparison, where individuals are constantly comparing their lives to others. This can lead to feelings of inadequacy, jealousy, and anxiety. Social media influencers, in particular, can create unrealistic expectations and perpetuate a culture of materialism and consumerism.

4. Online Impersonation: Social media has made it easier for individuals to create fake profiles and impersonate others. This can lead to online harassment, identity theft, and other forms of cybercrime.

5. Social Pressure: Social media can create a sense of social pressure, where individuals feel the need to conform to the norms and values of their online community. This can lead to self-censorship and a reluctance to express unpopular opinions.

6. Online Activism: While social media can be a powerful tool for social change, it can also lead to armchair activism, where individuals feel like they are making a difference by sharing posts and liking content, without taking any real-world action.

7. Information Overload: Social media can create a sense of information overload, where individuals are bombarded with a constant stream of news, updates, and notifications. This can lead to cognitive overload and a decrease in attention span.

The social media dilemma is a complex issue that involves

multiple dimensions, including privacy concerns, filter bubbles, comparison culture, online impersonation, social pressure, online activism, and information overload. It is essential to be aware of these issues and take proactive steps to mitigate their negative impact on our lives.

Explanation of the social media dilemma

The social media dilemma refers to the negative impact that social media can have on our mental health, social relationships, and society as a whole. Social media platforms have become an integral part of our daily lives, but they can also be addictive, manipulative, and harmful.

One of the main concerns with social media is the persuasive techniques used by these platforms to keep users engaged. Social media companies use algorithms to track user behavior and tailor the user experience to keep users on the platform for longer periods. This can lead to social media addiction, where individuals spend excessive amounts of time on social media, impacting their productivity, mental health, and overall well-being.

Another issue with social media is the impact it can have on mental health. Studies have shown that excessive use of social media can contribute to feelings of anxiety, depression, and loneliness. Social media can create unrealistic expectations and comparisons, leading to negative self-image and self-esteem. Cyberbullying, trolling, and harassment are also common on social media platforms, leading to emotional distress and psychological harm.

Social media can also have a significant impact on social relationships. While social media has made it easier to connect with others, it can also lead to social isolation and loneliness. Social media can create a false sense of connection, where individuals feel like they are connected to others, but in reality, they are only connected through a screen. This can lead to a lack of meaningful human interaction and a deterioration of in-person social relationships.

Finally, social media can have a significant impact on society as a whole. Social media can be used as a tool for spreading misinformation, propaganda, and fake news, impacting public opinion and the democratic process. Social media can also be used to amplify hate speech, incite violence, and promote extremist ideologies, leading to social unrest and division.

In summary, the social media dilemma refers to the complex challenges and risks associated with the use of social media. While social media has brought many benefits, it has also contributed to social, psychological, and societal problems. It is essential to be aware of the social media dilemma and take proactive steps to reduce its negative impact on our lives.

Here are some additional elements that can be added to the explanation of the social media dilemma:

1. Privacy Concerns: Social media platforms collect vast amounts of user data, including personal information, search history, and online behavior. This data can be used for targeted advertising and even sold to third parties. Many users are unaware of how their data is being used, leading to concerns about privacy and data security.

2. Filter Bubbles: Social media algorithms are designed to

show users content that is most relevant to them, based on their past behavior and preferences. This can lead to the creation of filter bubbles, where users only see content that reinforces their existing beliefs and opinions. This can lead to a lack of exposure to diverse viewpoints and a narrowing of the user's worldview.

3. Comparison Culture: Social media can create a culture of comparison, where individuals are constantly comparing their lives to others. This can lead to feelings of inadequacy, jealousy, and anxiety. Social media influencers, in particular, can create unrealistic expectations and perpetuate a culture of materialism and consumerism.

4. Online Impersonation: Social media has made it easier for individuals to create fake profiles and impersonate others. This can lead to online harassment, identity theft, and other forms of cybercrime.

5. Social Pressure: Social media can create a sense of social pressure, where individuals feel the need to conform to the norms and values of their online community. This can lead to self-censorship and a reluctance to express unpopular opinions.

6. Online Activism: While social media can be a powerful tool for social change, it can also lead to armchair activism, where individuals feel like they are making a difference by sharing posts and liking content, without taking any real-world action.

7. Information Overload: Social media can create a sense of information overload, where individuals are bombarded with a constant stream of news, updates, and notifications. This can lead to cognitive overload and a decrease in attention span.

In conclusion, the social media dilemma is a complex issue that involves multiple dimensions, including privacy concerns, filter bubbles, comparison culture, online impersonation, social pressure, online activism, and information overload. It is essential to be aware of these issues and take proactive steps to mitigate their negative impact on our lives.

Overview of the book's objective

The objective of "The Social Dilemma: How Social Media is Hijacking Our Minds and What We Can Do About It" is to provide readers with a comprehensive understanding of the challenges and risks associated with social media use, and to offer practical solutions for mitigating its negative impact.

The book aims to educate readers about the persuasive techniques used by social media platforms to keep users engaged and addicted, and to raise awareness about the impact of excessive social media use on mental health, social relationships, and society as a whole. The book also explores the privacy concerns, filter bubbles, comparison culture, online impersonation, social pressure, online activism, and information overload that contribute to the social media dilemma.

By providing a comprehensive overview of the social media dilemma, the book aims to empower readers to make informed decisions about their social media use and to take proactive steps to reduce its negative impact on their lives. The book provides practical tips and strategies for minimizing social media use, cultivating healthy social relationships, improving mental health and well-being, and promoting digital literacy and media literacy skills.

The objective of the book is to promote a critical and reflective approach to social media use and to encourage readers to become more mindful and intentional in their online behavior. The book ultimately seeks to empower readers to take control of their digital lives and to create a more balanced and fulfilling relationship with social media.

Brief history of social media

Social media has its roots in early forms of online communication such as bulletin board systems (BBS) and Usenet, which emerged in the late 1970s and 1980s. These early platforms allowed users to communicate and share information with others in a virtual environment.

The first true social media platform was Six Degrees, which launched in 1997. Six Degrees allowed users to create profiles, connect with friends, and send messages. Other early social media platforms included Friendster, MySpace, and LinkedIn, which launched in the early 2000s.

However, it was Facebook that revolutionized social media, launching in 2004 as a platform exclusively for college students. Facebook quickly expanded to other universities, and eventually to the general public, becoming the dominant social media platform of the 2000s.

Other social media platforms emerged in the late 2000s and early 2010s, including Twitter, Instagram, Snapchat, and Pinterest. These platforms focused on specific types of content, such as short-form messaging (Twitter), photo sharing (Instagram), and visual bookmarking (Pinterest).

Social media has since become an integral part of everyday

life, with billions of users around the world connecting and sharing information on a daily basis. Social media has transformed the way we communicate, socialize, and consume information, and has had a profound impact on politics, culture, and society as a whole.

As social media platforms gained popularity in the 2000s and 2010s, they became more diverse and specialized, catering to different audiences and purposes. Twitter, for example, emerged as a platform for short-form messaging, allowing users to post updates of up to 140 characters. Instagram, on the other hand, focused on photo sharing and visual storytelling, allowing users to upload and share photos and videos.

Snapchat, which launched in 2011, introduced the concept of ephemeral messaging, allowing users to send photos and videos that disappear after a short period of time. This concept was quickly adopted by other platforms, including Instagram and Facebook.

In addition to these social media platforms, there are also niche platforms that cater to specific interests and communities. LinkedIn, for example, is a professional networking platform that allows users to connect with colleagues and potential employers. Reddit is a platform for online discussion and sharing of content, organized into different topic-based communities called subreddits.

Social media has had a profound impact on society, shaping the way we communicate, socialize, and consume information. It has enabled people to connect with others across the globe, and has facilitated the spread of information and ideas. Social media has also played a role in political movements and activism, allowing people to organize and mobilize around social and political issues.

However, social media has also been criticized for its negative effects, including the spread of misinformation, cyberbullying, and the impact on mental health. Social media addiction has become a growing concern, with many users struggling to disconnect from their devices and the constant barrage of information and notifications.

As social media continues to evolve and shape our lives, it is important to understand its history and impact, as well as its potential risks and benefits.

Significant impact of social Media

One of the most significant impacts of social media has been its role in transforming the media landscape. Traditional media outlets, such as newspapers and television, have been challenged by the rise of social media, which has enabled citizen journalism and the sharing of information and news stories in real-time. Social media has given a platform to marginalized voices and has facilitated the democratization of news.

However, the proliferation of fake news, clickbait, and sensationalism on social media has also led to a crisis of trust in traditional media and has raised concerns about the accuracy and reliability of news sources. Social media algorithms, which prioritize engagement and virality, have been criticized for promoting sensational and divisive content, and for creating filter bubbles that reinforce users' existing beliefs and opinions.

Another impact of social media has been on the economy, with social media platforms becoming a major source of revenue for companies and advertisers. Social media advertising has become highly targeted, based on user data and behavior, and has enabled companies to reach specific demographics with precision.

However, the monetization of social media has also raised concerns about privacy and data security. Social media platforms collect vast amounts of user data, including personal information and online behavior, which can be sold to third-party advertisers and used for targeted advertising. The Cambridge Analytica scandal in 2018, which revealed that user data was harvested and used for political purposes, highlighted the need for stronger regulations and protections for user data.

Finally, social media has also had a significant impact on the way we perceive ourselves and others. The constant comparison culture and pressure to present a perfect image on social media has been linked to negative effects on self-esteem and body image. Social media has also been criticized for contributing to online harassment and bullying, and for creating an unrealistic portrayal of life that can lead to feelings of inadequacy and dissatisfaction.

Social media is a complex and multifaceted phenomenon that has transformed the way we live, work, and interact with each other. While it has many benefits, it also has its risks and challenges, and it is important to understand these in order to use social media in a responsible and mindful way.

Chapter 2: How Social Media Works

Social media is a broad term used to describe web-based platforms and applications that allow users to create, share, and interact with content and other users.

Social media platforms operate on a model that allows users to create and share content, and the platform curates the content and distributes it to other users based on their interests and behavior.

Here are some key elements of how social media works:

Social Media Algorithms:

Social media algorithms are complex sets of rules and calculations that determine which content users see on their feeds. These algorithms use data such as a user's behavior, interests, and interactions with content to determine what to show them next.

The algorithms are designed to keep users engaged on the platform for longer by showing them content that is relevant and interesting to them. Algorithms are used by all major social media platforms, including Facebook, Twitter, Instagram, TikTok, and LinkedIn.

Content Creation:

Social media platforms allow users to create a wide variety of content, including text, images, videos, and links. Each platform has different rules and guidelines for what type of content is allowed.

For example, Facebook prohibits content that promotes hate speech, violence, or misinformation, while Instagram has rules around sexually explicit content and nudity. Social media platforms use automated systems and human moderators to detect and remove content that violates their policies.

Social Interaction:

Social media is built around social interaction. Users can follow or friend other users, join groups or communities, and send private messages. They can also like, share, and comment on content created by others. Social media platforms have become a way for people to connect and communicate with others who share similar interests or backgrounds. This has led to the creation of online communities centered around specific topics, such as food, travel, or politics.

Monetization:

Social media platforms make money by monetizing user data and content. They collect data on users' behavior and interests, which they use to serve targeted advertisements. Platforms also allow users to promote their content and reach a larger audience through paid advertising. Advertisers can target their ads based on factors such as age, gender, location, and interests. The more data social media platforms collect, the more valuable they become to advertisers.

Analytics and Metrics:

Social media platforms provide users with analytics and metrics to track the performance of their content and interactions. Users can see data such as how many likes, shares, and comments their posts receive, and which posts are most popular. This data can help users tailor their content to their audience and improve their engagement. Social media analytics are also used by businesses and marketers to track the performance of their social media campaigns.

Privacy and Security:
Social media platforms collect a significant amount of data on users, including personal information such as name, age, and location. This data is often used to serve targeted advertisements, but it can also be vulnerable to hacks and breaches. Social media platforms have faced criticism for their handling of user data and for not doing enough to protect user privacy and security. As a result, many platforms have updated their privacy policies and added additional security measures such as two-factor authentication.

Influencers:
Social media has given rise to a new type of celebrity known as influencers. Influencers are individuals who have built large followings on social media platforms and are able to influence their followers' behavior and purchasing decisions. Brands often partner with influencers to promote their products or services to their followers. This has led to the growth of influencer marketing as a major industry.

Viral Content:
Social media platforms are known for their ability to make

content go viral. Viral content is content that spreads quickly and widely across the internet. Social media platforms have made it easier for content to go viral by allowing users to share and repost content with their followers. Viral content can take many forms, such as memes, videos, or articles. When content goes viral, it can have a significant impact on society and culture.

Social Media Regulation:

Social media platforms are largely unregulated, but there is increasing pressure from governments and society to hold them accountable for the content that is posted on their platforms. Social media platforms have faced criticism for their role in spreading misinformation, hate speech, and extremist content. Some governments have passed laws regulating social media platforms, while others are considering doing so. Social media platforms have also implemented their own policies and guidelines to address these issues.

Social media works by creating a virtual space where users can create and share content, interact with others, and receive personalized content based on their behavior and interests. Social media platforms have become an integral part of modern communication and play a significant role in shaping our behavior, culture, and society.

Understanding how social media works is important for users to make informed decisions about their use of these platforms and for policymakers to create effective regulations. As social media continues to evolve, it will be important to continue to study its impact on society and culture.

Explanation of the social media algorithms

Social media algorithms are complex sets of rules and calculations used by social media platforms to determine what content users see on their feeds. These algorithms are designed to keep users engaged on the platform for longer by showing them content that is relevant and interesting to them.

Each social media platform has its own algorithm, but they all have some common elements. First, the algorithm collects data about a user's behavior, interests, and interactions with content. This data includes things like the posts they've liked, shared, or commented on, the profiles they've followed, and the content they've created.

Once the algorithm has collected this data, it uses it to determine what content to show the user next. The algorithm analyzes the data to identify patterns and make predictions about what content the user is likely to be interested in. For example, if a user has interacted with a lot of posts about cooking, the algorithm might show them more cooking-related content.

The algorithm also takes into account other factors when deciding what content to show a user. These factors can include the recency of the content, the popularity of the content, and the engagement it has received. The algorithm might show a user a popular post from a few days ago if it thinks the user will be interested in it.

Another important factor in social media algorithms is the user's network. The algorithm takes into account the content that the user's friends or followers have interacted with and shows them similar content. This creates a feedback loop where users are shown content that their network is also engaging with, which can reinforce certain beliefs or behaviors.

Finally, social media algorithms are constantly evolving. Platforms are always testing and tweaking their algorithms to improve engagement and keep users on the platform for longer. This can lead to changes in the types of content that are shown to users and the way that content is ranked.

Social media algorithms are complex systems that use data and predictions to determine what content users see on their feeds. While they can help keep users engaged with the platform, they can also reinforce certain beliefs or behaviors and lead to a filter bubble effect.

How these algorithms impact our behavior

Social media algorithms have a profound impact on our behavior, influencing what we see, how we feel, and what we do on social media platforms.

One of the ways that algorithms impact our behavior is through the creation of a filter bubble. Social media platforms use algorithms to curate our feeds by showing us content that they believe we will find interesting based on our past behavior, such as the content we have liked, commented on, or shared. This leads to a reinforcement of our existing beliefs and perspectives, as we are more likely to see content that confirms our pre-existing biases and less likely to encounter information that challenges them.

Over time, the filter bubble created by social media algorithms can contribute to the polarization of our beliefs and opinions. We become less exposed to diverse perspectives, and more susceptible to confirmation bias, the tendency to seek out and interpret information in a way that confirms our existing beliefs.

Another way that social media algorithms can impact our behavior is by influencing our emotions. Platforms are designed to keep us engaged and active by showing us content that is likely to elicit a strong emotional response, such as anger, sadness, or joy. When we engage with emotionally charged content, our brains release neurotransmitters like dopamine and oxytocin, which reinforce our engagement and motivate us to seek out more content that elicits a similar emotional response.

This can have both positive and negative consequences. On the one hand, social media can provide a sense of social support and validation, fostering feelings of connection and belonging. On the other hand, it can contribute to negative emotions like anxiety and depression, particularly when users are exposed to emotionally charged content that is distressing or triggering.

Finally, social media algorithms can also impact our behavior by influencing our actions and decision-making. By using data on our past behavior and preferences, algorithms can predict what types of content, products, or services we are likely to engage with and tailor their recommendations accordingly. This can lead to personalized advertising and marketing that is highly effective in driving user engagement and consumption.

However, it can also lead to unintended consequences. For example, social media algorithms have been accused of contributing to the spread of fake news and misinformation, by promoting sensationalist content that is more likely to be shared widely. Additionally, algorithms that prioritize engagement over accuracy can create echo chambers of like-minded individuals, who may be more susceptible to believing and spreading misinformation.

Social media algorithms have a significant impact on our behavior, influencing our beliefs, emotions, and actions. While they can be powerful tools for personalization and engagement, they also have the potential to create unintended consequences, such as the reinforcement of biases and the spread of misinformation. It is important for users to be aware of the ways in which algorithms shape their experiences on social media and to take steps to mitigate their negative effects.

Social media addiction and its effects

Social media addiction is a growing concern as more people spend increasing amounts of time on social media platforms. While social media can provide a sense of social connectedness and entertainment, excessive use can have negative effects on mental health and social functioning.

One of the most common effects of social media addiction is a decrease in productivity. Social media can be highly engaging, with its endless stream of content and notifications that keep users constantly distracted. As a result, many people find spending excessive amounts of time on social media, often at the expense of other important activities such as work, school, or personal relatiothemselvesnships.

Social media addiction can also have negative effects on mental health. Studies have shown that excessive social media use is associated with higher levels of anxiety, depression, and loneliness. This may be due to the unrealistic and curated nature of social media, which can lead to feelings of inadequacy or social comparison. The constant barrage of information and stimulation can also lead to cognitive overload and decision fatigue, making it difficult to focus or make meaningful connections with others.

Another effect of social media addiction is a decrease in social functioning. While social media can provide a sense of social connectedness, it can also be a poor substitute for real-world relationships. Excessive social media use can lead to social isolation, as users may prioritize online connections over in-person interactions. This can lead to a range of negative outcomes, including decreased self-esteem, a lack of empathy, and difficulty forming and maintaining real-world relationships.

In addition to these effects, social media addiction can also have physical consequences, such as disrupted sleep patterns and increased sedentary behavior. Over time, these can contribute to a range of health problems, including obesity, cardiovascular disease, and diabetes.

Social media addiction can have a range of negative effects on mental and physical health, as well as social functioning. While social media can provide many benefits, it is important to use it in moderation and to be mindful of its potential negative consequences. If you or someone you know is struggling with social media addiction, seeking professional help or support from friends and family can be an important first step in overcoming this challenge.

Chapter 3: The Power of Persuasion

Persuasion is the ability to convince someone to adopt a particular opinion, belief, or course of action. It is a powerful tool that can be used in a variety of settings, from personal relationships to marketing and advertising. Understanding the psychology of persuasion can help individuals and businesses become more effective at influencing others.

One of the key elements of persuasion is understanding the audience. Persuasion is most effective when the message is tailored to the needs and interests of the person or group being persuaded. This means taking the time to understand their perspective, values, and motivations, and framing the message in a way that resonates with them.

Another important factor in persuasion is credibility. People are more likely to be persuaded by someone they perceive as trustworthy and knowledgeable. Building credibility can be achieved through expertise, experience, or by using trusted sources and data to support the argument.

The use of emotion is also a powerful tool in persuasion. Emotional appeals can tap into feelings of empathy, fear, or desire, and can be a highly effective way to influence behavior.

For example, an advertisement for a product may use images of happy and satisfied customers to tap into a desire for social connection and approval.

Another tactic commonly used in persuasion is social proof. This refers to the idea that people are more likely to adopt a particular behavior or belief if they see others doing the same. Social proof can be leveraged through the use of testimonials, endorsements, or by highlighting the popularity or success of a particular product or idea.

Finally, the timing and context of the message can also play a role in persuasion. Messages that are delivered at the right time, in the right place, and to the right audience are more likely to be effective. For example, a message promoting a product or idea may be more effective if it is delivered during a time when the audience is already receptive, such as during a holiday season or special event.

The power of persuasion lies in the ability to understand and connect with the audience, build credibility, tap into emotions, use social proof, and deliver the message at the right time and place. By mastering these elements, individuals and businesses can become more effective at influencing behavior and achieving their goals.

There are several other factors that can impact the power of persuasion. These include:

1. Consistency: People are more likely to be persuaded if message is consistent with their existing beliefs and values. This is known as the principle of consistency, which suggests that people have a natural tendency to behave

in ways that are consistent with their past behavior and beliefs.

2. Authority: People are more likely to be persuaded by someone who is perceived as an authority figure or expert in a particular field. This can be achieved through credentials, experience, or other markers of expertise.

3. Scarcity: People are more likely to value something that is perceived as rare or in short supply. This principle can be used to create a sense of urgency and motivate people to take action.

4. Reciprocity: People are more likely to be persuaded by someone who has done something for them in the past. This principle suggests that people have a natural tendency to repay kindness or favors with kindness or favors of their own.

5. Framing: The way a message is framed can have a significant impact on its persuasive power. For example, a message that emphasizes the benefits of a particular action may be more effective than one that focuses on the risks or drawbacks.

6. Appeal to self-interest: People are more likely to be persuaded if they perceive that the message is in their own self-interest. Messages that emphasize the personal benefits of a particular action or belief are more likely to be persuasive than those that focus on broader societal benefits.

By understanding these additional elements of persuasion, individuals and businesses can become even more effective at influencing behavior and achieving their goals. However, it is important to use these tactics ethically and responsibly, and to be mindful of the potential consequences of using persuasion to achieve one's objectives.

Understanding the persuasive techniques used by social media platforms

Social media platforms are designed to be engaging and addictive, and they use a variety of persuasive techniques to keep users coming back for more. Some of the most common persuasive techniques used by social media platforms include:

1. Personalization: Social media platforms use personalization to tailor the user experience to each individual. This can include customized content recommendations, personalized notifications, and targeted advertising. By providing a personalized experience, social media platforms can create a sense of familiarity and connection with users, which can make them more likely to engage with the platform.

2. Social Proof: Social proof is the principle that people are more likely to adopt a particular behavior or belief if they see others doing the same. Social media platforms use social proof to create a sense of community and validation for users. For example, likes, comments, and shares on posts can provide social proof that the content is worth engaging with.

3. Scarcity: Social media platforms use scarcity to create a sense of urgency and motivate users to take action. This can include limited-time offers, exclusive content, or notifications that create a sense of FOMO (fear of missing

out). By creating a sense of scarcity, social media platforms can encourage users to engage with the platform more frequently and for longer periods of time.

4. Reciprocity: Social media platforms use reciprocity to encourage users to engage with the platform and with each other. For example, platforms may offer rewards or incentives for completing certain actions, such as sharing a post or inviting friends to join. By offering these rewards, social media platforms can create a sense of obligation and reciprocity that motivates users to engage with the platform more frequently.

5. Emotional Appeals: Social media platforms use emotional appeals to create a strong emotional connection with users. This can include using images or videos that evoke powerful emotions, such as happiness, nostalgia, or sadness. By creating an emotional connection, social media platforms can make users more invested in the platform and more likely to engage with it.

Social media platforms use a combination of persuasive techniques to create a highly engaging and addictive user experience. While these techniques can be highly effective, they can also have negative effects on mental health, well-being, and privacy. It is important for users to be aware of these techniques and to use social media in a way that is healthy and balanced.

The psychology of social media persuasion

Social media platforms are constantly evolving and refining their persuasive techniques to keep users engaged and active on their platforms. To better understand the psychology of social media persuasion, it is helpful to explore some of the specific techniques and strategies that these platforms use:

- Social proof: Social proof is the principle that people are more likely to adopt a particular behavior or belief if they see others doing the same. Social media platforms use social proof to create a sense of community and validation for users. For example, the number of likes, comments, and shares on a post can provide social proof that the content is worth engaging with.
- Reciprocity: Social media platforms use reciprocity to encourage users to engage with the platform and with each other. For example, platforms may offer rewards or incentives for completing certain actions, such as sharing a post or inviting friends to join. By offering these rewards, social media platforms can create a sense of obligation and reciprocity that motivates users to engage with the platform more frequently.
- Personalization: Social media platforms use personalization to tailor the user experience to each individual. This can include customized content recommendations, personalized notifications, and targeted advertising. By providing a personalized experience, social media platforms can create a sense of familiarity and connection with users, which can make them more likely to engage with the platform.

- Emotional appeals: Social media platforms use emotional appeals to create a strong emotional connection with users. This can include using images or videos that evoke powerful emotions, such as happiness, nostalgia, or sadness. By creating an emotional connection, social media platforms can make users more invested in the platform and more likely to engage with it.

- Algorithmic bias: Social media algorithms are designed to show users content that they are most likely to engage with. However, these algorithms can also be biased and reinforce existing beliefs and attitudes. For example, if a user tends to engage with content that supports a particular political viewpoint, the algorithm may prioritize similar content, reinforcing the user's existing beliefs and potentially creating a filter bubble.

- Fear of missing out (FOMO): Social media platforms use FOMO to create a sense of urgency and motivate users to take action. This can include limited-time offers, exclusive content, or notifications that create a sense of FOMO. By creating a sense of scarcity, social media platforms can encourage users to engage with the platform more frequently and for longer periods of time.

- Cognitive biases: Social media platforms can exploit cognitive biases to influence user behavior. For example, the availability bias (the tendency to overestimate the importance of information that is easily available) can be exploited by social media algorithms to prioritize certain types of content in users' feeds. Other cognitive biases that can be exploited by social media platforms include confirmation bias (the tendency to seek out information that confirms existing beliefs) and the sunk cost fallacy (the tendency to continue investing in something because of the resources already invested).

While social media platforms use these persuasive techniques to create a more engaging and addictive user experience, these techniques can also have negative effects on mental health, well-being, and privacy. It is important for users to be aware of these techniques and to use social media in a way that is healthy and balanced.

Examples of persuasive tactics used by social media platforms

Here are some examples of persuasive tactics used by social media platforms:

1. Notifications: Social media platforms use notifications to prompt users to engage with the platform. Notifications can be personalized and targeted to specific users, and they can be designed to create a sense of urgency or FOMO.
2. Likes and comments: Social media platforms use likes and comments as a form of social proof. Users are more likely to engage with content that has a high number of likes and comments, which can create a cycle of engagement that keeps users coming back to the platform.
3. Recommendations: Social media platforms use recommendation algorithms to suggest content to users that they are likely to engage with. These recommendations can be based on a user's past behavior, such as content they have liked or shared, and they can be designed to

keep users on the platform for longer periods of time.

4. Gamification: Social media platforms use gamification to make the user experience more engaging and addictive. This can include rewards for completing certain actions, such as sharing a post or inviting friends to join the platform, as well as badges or achievements that users can earn for reaching certain milestones.

5. Personalization: Social media platforms use personalization to tailor the user experience to each individual. This can include customized content recommendations, personalized notifications, and targeted advertising. By providing a personalized experience, social media platforms can create a sense of familiarity and connection with users, which can make them more likely to engage with the platform.

6. Influencer marketing: Social media platforms use influencer marketing to promote products and services to users. Influencers are individuals who have a large following on social media and are able to promote products or services to their followers. By using influencers, social media platforms can leverage the social proof of the influencer's following to create a sense of credibility and trust around the products or services being promoted.

7. Emotional appeals: Social media platforms use emotional appeals to create a strong emotional connection with users. This can include using images or videos that evoke powerful emotions, such as happiness, nostalgia, or sadness. By creating an emotional connection, social media platforms can make users more invested in the platform and more likely to engage with it.

It is important to note that while these persuasive tactics can make the user experience more engaging and addictive, they can also have negative effects on mental health, well-being, and privacy. It is important for users to be aware of these tactics and to use social media in a way that is healthy and balanced.

CHAPTER 4: THE IMPACT OF SOCIAL MEDIA ON MENTAL HEALTH

The impact of social media on mental health has been a topic of concern for many researchers and mental health professionals in recent years. Here are some ways that social media can impact mental health:

- Social comparison: Social media platforms can contribute to feelings of social comparison, which can negatively impact mental health. Users may compare their lives to the curated and often idealized versions of others' lives that are portrayed on social media, leading to feelings of inadequacy and self-doubt.
- Cyberbullying: Social media platforms can be a breeding ground for cyberbullying, which can have a significant impact on mental health. Cyberbullying can include harassment, threats, and rumors, and can lead to feelings of anxiety, depression, and social isolation.
- Addiction: Social media use can become addictive, leading to compulsive and excessive use that can negatively impact mental health. Addiction to social media can lead to decreased productivity, sleep disturbances, and other negative effects on mental health.
- Sleep disturbances: The use of social media before bed can contribute to sleep disturbances, which can negatively

impact mental health. The blue light emitted by electronic devices can disrupt the body's natural sleep-wake cycle, leading to difficulty falling asleep and poor sleep quality.

- Fear of missing out (FOMO): Social media can contribute to feelings of FOMO, which can negatively impact mental health. Users may feel pressure to constantly check social media to avoid missing out on important events or updates, leading to feelings of anxiety and stress.

- Reduced self-esteem: Social media can contribute to reduced self-esteem, particularly among young people. The pressure to present a certain image on social media can lead to feelings of inadequacy and self-doubt, which can negatively impact mental health.

It is important to note that while social media can have negative impacts on mental health, it can also be a source of support and connection for individuals who use it in a healthy and balanced way. It is important for individuals to be aware of the potential negative impacts of social media and to use it in a way that promotes mental health and well-being.

The correlation between social media and mental health problems

There is a growing body of research that suggests a correlation between social media use and mental health problems. Here are some ways that social media can impact mental health:

1. Anxiety and depression: Studies have found that heavy social media use is associated with higher rates of anxiety

and depression. This may be due to the pressure to present a certain image on social media, as well as the potential for cyberbullying and social comparison.

2. Body image issues: Social media platforms can contribute to body image issues, particularly among young people. The idealized and often unrealistic images that are portrayed on social media can lead to feelings of inadequacy and self-doubt.

3. Sleep disturbances: The use of social media before bed can contribute to sleep disturbances, which can negatively impact mental health. The blue light emitted by electronic devices can disrupt the body's natural sleep-wake cycle, leading to difficulty falling asleep and poor sleep quality.

4. Addiction: Social media use can become addictive, leading to compulsive and excessive use that can negatively impact mental health. Addiction to social media can lead to decreased productivity, sleep disturbances, and other negative effects on mental health.

5. Social isolation: While social media can be a source of connection, it can also contribute to social isolation. Studies have found that heavy social media use is associated with lower levels of in-person social interactions, which can lead to feelings of loneliness and isolation.

6. Self-esteem issues: Social media can contribute to reduced self-esteem, particularly among young people. The pressure to present a certain image on social media can lead to feelings of inadequacy and self-doubt, which can negatively impact mental health.

It is important to note that correlation does not necessarily equal causation, and more research is needed to fully understand the relationship between social media use and mental health problems. However, it is clear that social media can have negative impacts on mental health, particularly when used in a way that is excessive or unhealthy. It is important for individuals to be aware of the potential negative impacts of social media and to use it in a way that promotes mental health and well-being.

The rise of social media addiction and its effects on mental health

Social media addiction is a growing problem that can have negative effects on mental health. Here are some ways that social media addiction can impact mental health:

1. Anxiety and depression: People who are addicted to social media may experience higher levels of anxiety and depression. This may be due to the pressure to constantly check notifications, the fear of missing out (FOMO), and the potential for cyberbullying and social comparison.
2. Decreased productivity: Social media addiction can lead to decreased productivity at work or school, which can negatively impact mental health by increasing stress and feelings of inadequacy.
3. Sleep disturbances: Addiction to social media can lead to sleep disturbances, which can negatively impact mental health. People who are addicted to social media may stay up late scrolling through their feeds, leading to difficulty falling asleep and poor sleep quality.
4. Relationship problems: Social media addiction can lead

to relationship problems, as people may prioritize social media over in-person interactions. This can lead to feelings of loneliness and isolation, which can negatively impact mental health.

5. Self-esteem issues: Addiction to social media can lead to reduced self-esteem, particularly among young people. The pressure to present a certain image on social media can lead to feelings of inadequacy and self-doubt, which can negatively impact mental health.

6. Physical health problems: Addiction to social media can lead to physical health problems, such as eye strain, headaches, and neck pain. These physical health problems can contribute to feelings of stress and anxiety, which can negatively impact mental health.

It is important for individuals to be aware of the signs of social media addiction and to seek help if necessary. Treatment for social media addiction may include therapy, behavioral interventions, and limiting or monitoring social media use. By taking steps to reduce social media addiction, individuals can improve their mental health and overall well-being.

Social comparison and its impact on mental health

Social comparison is the tendency to compare oneself to others, particularly on social media. Social media platforms are designed to facilitate social comparison, as users can easily see the highlights of other people's lives and compare them to their own. Here are some ways that social comparison can impact mental health:

- Decreased self-esteem: When people compare themselves to others on social media, they may feel like they don't measure up. This can lead to decreased self-esteem and negative feelings about oneself.
- FOMO: Social comparison can also lead to a fear of missing out (FOMO) on experiences that others are having. This can cause anxiety and stress, particularly among young people.
- Negative body image: Social media is full of images of "perfect" bodies, which can lead to negative body image and disordered eating behaviors. People may feel pressure to look a certain way in order to fit in with the images they see on social media.
- Anxiety and depression: Social comparison can lead to anxiety and depression, particularly among people who are already prone to these conditions. People who compare themselves to others on social media may feel like they don't measure up, which can lead to feelings of worthlessness and hopelessness.
- Relationship problems: Social comparison can also lead to relationship problems, particularly in romantic relationships. People may compare their relationship to others they see on social media, which can lead to feelings of jealousy and insecurity.

To combat the negative effects of social comparison on mental health, it's important to be mindful of one's social media use. This may involve taking breaks from social media, limiting time spent on social media, or unfollowing accounts that trigger negative feelings. It's also important to remember that social media only shows a small slice of people's lives, and that people often present a curated version of themselves online. By focusing on one's own strengths and accomplishments, rather than comparing oneself to others, individuals can improve their mental health and well-being.

The impact of cyberbullying on mental health

CYBERBULLYING

Cyberbullying refers to the use of technology, such as social media, texting, and instant messaging, to harass, intimidate, or embarrass someone. Cyberbullying can take many forms, including sending threatening messages, spreading rumors online, or posting embarrassing photos or videos.

The impact of cyberbullying on mental health can be significant. Here are some ways that cyberbullying can affect mental health:

1. Anxiety and Depression: Cyberbullying can lead to feelings of anxiety and depression, particularly if the victim feels isolated or powerless to stop the bullying. Victims may also feel ashamed or embarrassed, which can exacerbate these feelings.
2. Self-Esteem: Cyberbullying can damage a victim's self-esteem, particularly if the bullying involves negative comments about the victim's appearance, intelligence, or other personal characteristics.
3. Social Isolation: Cyberbullying can cause victims to withdraw from social situations, particularly if the bullying occurs online in front of others. Victims may feel like they can't trust anyone, which can lead to social isolation and

loneliness.

4. Physical Health: Cyberbullying can also impact physical health. Victims may experience headaches, stomachaches, and other physical symptoms as a result of the stress and anxiety caused by the bullying.

5. Self-Harm and Suicidal Thoughts: In extreme cases, cyberbullying can lead to self-harm and suicidal thoughts. Victims may feel like there is no escape from the bullying and that the only way out is to harm themselves or end their lives.

It's important to take cyberbullying seriously and to seek help if you or someone you know is being bullied online. Victims of cyberbullying should talk to a trusted adult, such as a teacher or counselor, and should also consider blocking the bully online and reporting the bullying to the social media platform or website where it is occurring. By taking action to stop cyberbullying, we can help prevent the negative impact it can have on mental health.

Chapter 5: The Impact of Social Media on Society

Social media has had a significant impact on society in various ways, both positive and negative. Here are some of the ways social media has impacted society:

1. Communication: Social media has revolutionized the way people communicate with each other. It has made it easier for people to connect with friends and family members who live far away, as well as to make new friends with similar interests. Social media has also made it easier for people to share news and information quickly and easily.

2. Business: Social media has transformed the way businesses operate. It has made it easier for businesses to reach out to customers and to market their products and services. Social media platforms such as Facebook, Twitter, and Instagram provide businesses with a way to engage with their customers and to build their brand.

3. Politics: Social media has had a profound impact on politics. It has made it easier for politicians to reach out to voters and to build a following. Social media platforms have also been used to organize political protests and to

raise awareness about social and political issues.

4. Mental Health: Social media has had a mixed impact on mental health. On the one hand, it has provided people with a way to connect with others and to build support networks. On the other hand, social media can also be a source of stress and anxiety, particularly when people feel pressured to present a perfect image of themselves online.

5. Privacy: Social media has raised concerns about privacy. Social media platforms collect a vast amount of personal data about users, which can be used for targeted advertising and other purposes. This has led to concerns about how this data is being used and who has access to it.

6. Cyberbullying: Social media has also been linked to cyberbullying, which can have a devastating impact on individuals and communities. Cyberbullying can cause psychological harm and can lead to social isolation and even suicide.

Social media has had a profound impact on society. While it has brought people together and provided new opportunities for communication and connection, it has also raised concerns about privacy, mental health, and cyberbullying. It is important for individuals, businesses, and policymakers to consider the impact of social media on society and to work to mitigate its negative effects.

The impact of social media on politics

Social media has had a significant impact on politics in recent years. Here are some of the ways social media has impacted politics:

- Political Campaigns: Social media platforms have become essential tools for political campaigns. Political candidates and parties use social media to reach out to voters, share their message, and build support. Social media allows political campaigns to target specific demographics and to reach a wider audience than traditional media.
- Mobilization: Social media has been used to mobilize voters and to encourage political participation. Political activists use social media to organize rallies and protests, to raise awareness about political issues, and to encourage people to vote.
- Political Discourse: Social media has transformed political discourse by providing a platform for individuals to express their opinions and engage in debates. Social media has given a voice to marginalized groups and has made it easier for people to connect with like-minded individuals.
- Disinformation: Social media has been linked to the spread of disinformation and fake news. Social media algorithms can amplify false or misleading information, making it difficult for people to distinguish between fact and fiction. This has led to concerns about the impact of social media on democracy and the ability of citizens to make informed decisions.
- Election Interference: Social media has been used to interfere in elections by foreign governments and other

actors. Social media platforms have been criticized for their role in allowing foreign interference in elections and for their handling of political ads and misinformation.

Social media has had a significant impact on politics. While it has provided new opportunities for political mobilization and engagement, it has also raised concerns about the spread of disinformation and election interference. It is important for policymakers to consider the impact of social media on politics and to work to address its negative effects.

The influence of social media on elections

Social media has had a significant influence on elections in recent years. Here are some of the ways social media has impacted elections:

- Campaign Advertising: Social media platforms have become essential tools for political campaigns to advertise their message and reach out to voters. Campaigns can target specific demographics and reach a wider audience than traditional media.
- Voter Mobilization: Social media has been used to mobilize voters and encourage political participation. Political activists use social media to organize rallies and protests, raise awareness about political issues, and encourage people to vote.
- Viral Content: Social media allows political content to go viral, potentially reaching millions of people quickly. This can be beneficial for campaigns with limited budgets and

can help to build support for political candidates and issues.

- Disinformation and Fake News: Social media has been linked to the spread of disinformation and fake news, which can be used to influence elections. Social media algorithms can amplify false or misleading information, making it difficult for people to distinguish between fact and fiction.
- Election Interference: Social media has been used to interfere in elections by foreign governments and other actors. Social media platforms have been criticized for their role in allowing foreign interference in elections and for their handling of political ads and misinformation.
- Opinion Polls: Social media has also been used for opinion polling and data gathering. By tracking and analyzing social media interactions, political campaigns can gain insights into the opinions and attitudes of voters.

Social media has had a significant impact on elections. While it has provided new opportunities for political mobilization and engagement, it has also raised concerns about the spread of disinformation and election interference. It is important for policymakers to consider the impact of social media on elections and to work to address its negative effects.

The impact of social media on social movements

Social media has had a significant impact on social movements, providing new opportunities for organizing, mobilizing and communicating with supporters. Here are some of the ways social media has impacted social movements:

- Amplifying Voices: Social media allows activists to amplify their voices and reach a wider audience than traditional media. Social media platforms have been used to share stories, images, and videos that shed light on social issues and build support for social movements.
- Mobilization: Social media has been used to mobilize people to participate in protests, rallies, and other forms of activism. Social media platforms have allowed activists to connect with like-minded individuals and build communities around shared goals.
- Fundraising: Social media platforms have been used to raise funds for social movements, providing a new way for activists to fund their work and reach a wider audience.
- Awareness-raising: Social media has been used to raise awareness about social issues and educate people about the causes of social movements. Activists have used social media platforms to share information about their cause and engage people in conversations about social justice.
- Accountability: Social media has been used to hold governments, corporations, and other powerful actors accountable for their actions. Activists have used social media platforms to expose corruption, human rights abuses, and other forms of injustice.

Social media has had a significant impact on social movements, providing new opportunities for organizing, mobilizing and communicating with supporters. However, social media has also posed new challenges for social movements, including the spread of misinformation, the risk of censorship, and the need to constantly adapt to changing platforms and algorithms. Despite these challenges, social media has become a critical tool for social movements seeking to effect change in society.

The role of social media in shaping cultural norms and values

Social media has become a powerful force in shaping cultural norms and values. Here are some ways in which social media is impacting cultural norms and values:

1. Spreading Cultural Awareness: Social media allows people to learn about different cultures, traditions, and customs from around the world. This can help to increase cultural awareness and promote tolerance and acceptance.

2. Influencing Popular Culture: Social media has a significant influence on popular culture, shaping what we watch, listen to, and read. Social media platforms like TikTok, Instagram, and YouTube have created new forms of entertainment and have become a platform for influencers to share their opinions and ideas.

3. Changing Social Norms: Social media has challenged traditional social norms and has helped to create new ones. Social media platforms have provided a platform for marginalized groups to share their stories and advocate for their rights, leading to changes in societal attitudes and beliefs.

4. Promoting Social Justice: Social media has played a critical role in promoting social justice issues, such as #MeToo, Black Lives Matter, and LGBTQ+ rights. Social media has helped to amplify the voices of activists and advocates, and has been used to mobilize people to take action and effect

change.

5. Creating a Global Community: Social media has created a global community where people from different cultures and backgrounds can connect and share their ideas and experiences. This has helped to break down barriers and promote understanding between people from different parts of the world.

Social media has become a powerful force in shaping cultural norms and values, both positively and negatively. While social media has helped to promote cultural awareness, social justice, and global understanding, it has also posed new challenges, including the spread of misinformation, the rise of cyberbullying, and the impact of social media on mental health. It is important to continue to examine and understand the impact of social media on cultural norms and values, and to work towards creating a more positive and inclusive online community.

Chapter 6: Privacy Concerns and Data Collection

P rivacy concerns and data collection are two related issues that have become increasingly relevant in the digital age. In today's digital landscape, individuals are becoming more aware of the amount of personal information that is being collected by various entities, including social media platforms. Here is a more comprehensive explanation of these topics:

Privacy Concerns:

Privacy concerns refer to the issues related to the collection, storage, use, and sharing of personal information by organizations or individuals. With the growth of social media platforms, individuals have become increasingly concerned about how their personal information is being used by these platforms. Social media platforms collect a large amount of personal information from their users, including their name, age, location, interests, and even their online behavior. This information can be used by the platforms to tailor advertisements, content, and recommendations to users. However, it can also be used by third parties to target users with ads, engage in surveillance or even commit cybercrimes. In addition to this, there is a concern about the potential misuse of personal information, including identity theft, financial fraud, or even reputational damage.

Data Collection:

Data collection is the process of gathering, processing, and storing information. Social media platforms collect data on users in many ways, including through their posts, messages, and search history. They also use tracking technologies such as cookies, pixels, and device identifiers to collect information on users' online behavior, including the websites they visit, the ads they click on, and their location. This information can be used by social media platforms to create detailed profiles of users and to tailor content and ads to their interests.

The collection and use of personal data by social media platforms has raised concerns about privacy, transparency, and accountability. Users are becoming more aware of their rights and the risks associated with sharing personal information online. To address these concerns, many social media platforms have implemented privacy policies and settings that allow users to control how their personal information is collected and shared. However, the effectiveness of these measures remains a matter of debate, and users must remain vigilant to protect their personal information.

Privacy concerns and data collection are two significant issues in today's digital landscape. Users should be aware of the information they share online and take steps to protect their personal information. Social media platforms must also take responsibility for the data they collect and ensure that their data collection practices are transparent and accountable. Finally, policymakers must create regulations that protect the privacy of users and ensure the responsible use of personal data by social media platforms.

Privacy concerns and data collection are major issues that have arisen with the increasing use of social media.

Here are some key points related to these issues:

1. Data Collection: Social media platforms collect vast amounts of data about their users, including personal information, search history, and online behavior. This data is often used for targeted advertising and to improve the user experience. However, there are concerns about how this data is collected, stored, and used, and whether users have given informed consent for this data to be collected.

2. Targeted Advertising: Social media platforms use the data they collect to deliver targeted advertising to users. While this can be beneficial for businesses, it also raises concerns about privacy, as users may feel that their personal information is being used without their knowledge or consent.

3. Cybersecurity: The data collected by social media platforms is often highly sensitive, and there are concerns about how secure this data is. Cybersecurity threats, such as data breaches and hacking, can compromise the privacy and security of users' personal information.

4. Surveillance: There are concerns that social media platforms are being used for surveillance purposes by governments and other organizations. This raises questions about privacy and civil liberties, as users may feel that their online activities are being monitored without their knowledge or consent.

5. Data Misuse: There have been cases where social media

platforms have been accused of misusing user data, such as the Cambridge Analytica scandal. This has led to increased scrutiny of social media companies and calls for greater regulation of data collection and use.

Privacy concerns and data collection are important issues that need to be addressed in the context of social media. Users need to be informed about how their data is being collected and used, and there needs to be greater transparency and accountability from social media companies. It is important to find a balance between the benefits of social media and the protection of users' privacy and security.

The Impact Of Social media On Personal Privacy

Social media has had a significant impact on personal privacy in recent years. With the increasing use of social media platforms, individuals are sharing more and more personal information online, leading to concerns about privacy and data security. Here are some of the ways that social media has impacted personal privacy:

1. Increased sharing of personal information: Social media platforms encourage users to share personal information, including their name, age, location, and interests. Users often share photos and updates about their personal lives, creating a digital footprint that can be accessed by others. This can lead to privacy concerns, as users may inadvertently share personal information that can be used to identify or target them.

2. Targeted advertising: Social media platforms use personal information to create targeted advertisements. Advertisers can use this information to create ads that are more likely to be relevant to the user. While some users may appreciate targeted advertising, others may feel that their privacy has been compromised.

3. Data breaches: Social media platforms have experienced numerous data breaches in recent years. Hackers have been able to access large amounts of personal information, including passwords, email addresses, and even credit card numbers. This can lead to identity theft and other privacy concerns.

4. Surveillance: Social media platforms can be used for surveillance purposes. Governments, law enforcement agencies, and even employers can monitor social media activity to track individuals or gather intelligence. This can lead to concerns about privacy and civil liberties.

5. Privacy settings: Most social media platforms offer privacy settings that allow users to control who can see their posts and personal information. However, these settings can be complicated and confusing, and many users may not understand how to use them effectively. This can lead to unintended sharing of personal information.

Social media has had a significant impact on personal privacy. While social media platforms offer many benefits, including the ability to connect with others and share information, users should be aware of the privacy risks associated with these platforms. To protect their privacy, users should carefully consider what information they share online, use privacy settings effectively, and be cautious about who they connect with online.

How Social Media Collects And Uses Data

Social media companies collect data from their users in various ways, including through their posts, likes, comments, shares, messages, and search history. They also collect data from other sources, such as third-party apps and websites, and device information such as IP address, browser type, operating system, and mobile carrier.

Social media platforms collect and use data in various ways, including. Here are some of the ways social media companies collect and use data:

- User-provided data: Social media platforms ask users to provide personal information when they create an account. This can include their name, age, gender, and location. Users may also choose to provide additional information, such as their interests or hobbies. This information is used to create a profile and to provide personalized content and advertising.
- User activity data: Social media platforms collect data on users' activity, such as the content they view, the posts they like and share, and the people they follow. This data is used to personalize content and advertising and to improve the user experience.
- Device and location data: Social media platforms collect data on the devices that users use to access their platforms, such as the type of device and operating system. They also collect location data, such as the user's IP address or GPS

location. This data is used to provide personalized content and advertising and to improve the user experience.

- Third-party data: Social media platforms may collect data from third-party sources, such as data brokers or advertisers. This data can include information about users' demographics, interests, and behavior. It is used to personalize content and advertising and to improve the user experience.

Social media platforms use this data in various ways, including:

- Advertising: Social media companies use data to show users targeted ads. They collect information about users' interests, behaviors, demographics, and location to create a profile of their preferences and show them relevant ads. Advertisers can use this data to target specific audiences with their ads.
- Personalization: Social media platforms use data to personalize content and advertising. For example, they may show users content and ads based on their interests, location, and activity.
- Analytics: Social media platforms use data to analyze user behavior and to improve the user experience. For example, they may use data to identify popular content or to improve the performance of their platforms.
- Ad targeting: Social media platforms use data to target ads to specific users. For example, they may show ads to users who have expressed interest in a particular product or service.
- Research: Social media platforms may use data for research

purposes, such as to identify trends or to improve their products.

It is important to note that social media platforms have access to a vast amount of personal information, and users should be aware of the data that is being collected and how it is being used. While some users may appreciate personalized content and advertising, others may feel uncomfortable with the level of data collection and targeted advertising. Social media platforms should be transparent about their data collection practices and allow users to control their data and privacy settings.

However, there are concerns over how social media companies collect and use data, particularly when it comes to users' privacy. Social media companies have been criticized for collecting data without users' consent and sharing it with third-party companies. Users may also be unaware of how their data is being used and have little control over it. As such, social media companies are facing increasing pressure to be transparent about their data collection practices and give users more control over their personal information.

The Dangers Of Data Collection And Misuse

The widespread collection of personal data by social media companies and other organizations has raised concerns about the potential dangers of data collection and misuse. Here are some of the dangers of data collection and misuse:

- Privacy violations: Collecting personal data without user consent can be a violation of privacy. Users may not be aware of the extent of data collected about them, or how it is being used or shared.

- Identity theft: Personal data such as names, addresses, and birth dates can be used by hackers to steal identities and commit fraud.
- Cyberbullying and harassment: Personal data collected on social media can be used to harass and bully users, which can have serious emotional and psychological impacts.
- Discrimination: Personal data can be used to discriminate against individuals based on characteristics such as race, gender, or sexual orientation.
- Political manipulation: Data collected from social media can be used to influence political opinions and elections.
- Health risks: Personal data collected by health tracking apps and wearables can be used to discriminate against individuals with pre-existing conditions, or to create inaccurate health profiles.
- Financial fraud: Personal data collected by financial institutions can be used to commit fraud or identity theft.

The misuse of personal data can have significant impacts on individuals and society as a whole. As such, it is important for individuals to be aware of how their data is being collected and used, and for organizations to implement appropriate data protection measures to prevent misuse.

The Role Of Social Media In Facilitating The Spread Of Misinformation

Social media has revolutionized the way we communicate and share information. While it has brought many benefits, it has also facilitated the spread of misinformation, which can have serious consequences. Here are some ways in which social media can spread misinformation:

- Viral content: Social media platforms are designed to encourage the sharing of content, which can lead to the rapid spread of false information.
- Algorithmic bias: Social media algorithms may promote certain types of content or sources over others, which can lead to the spread of biased or inaccurate information.
- Echo chambers: Social media can create echo chambers in which users are exposed only to information that confirms their pre-existing beliefs, which can lead to the spread of false information.
- Disinformation campaigns: Social media can be used to spread deliberate disinformation campaigns, which can be difficult to detect and combat.
- Lack of fact-checking: Social media platforms may not have effective mechanisms in place for fact-checking information, which can lead to the spread of false information.
- Lack of context: Social media posts may be taken out of context or presented in a misleading way, which can contribute to the spread of false information.

The spread of misinformation on social media can have serious consequences, such as undermining public trust in institutions, stoking political polarization, and even endangering public health. It is important for social media companies to take steps to combat the spread of misinformation, such as implementing fact-checking mechanisms, reducing algorithmic bias, and promoting media literacy. It is also important for individuals to be critical consumers of information, fact-checking information before sharing it and seeking out multiple sources to verify claims.

Chapter 7: Ethical Considerations for Social Media Companies

As social media continues to play an increasingly influential role in our lives, it has become imperative that the companies that operate these platforms adhere to high ethical standards. There are several ethical considerations that social media companies must take into account:

1. User Privacy: Social media companies must prioritize user privacy and ensure that they are protecting user data from misuse. They should be transparent about what data they collect and how they use it.

2. Content Moderation: Social media platforms must also take responsibility for the content that is posted on their sites. They must ensure that harmful content such as hate speech, incitement to violence, and misinformation are removed promptly and that the users who post such content are held accountable.

3. Algorithmic Transparency: Social media companies use algorithms to determine what content users see. These algorithms must be transparent and free from bias to avoid

promoting certain ideas or viewpoints at the expense of others.

4. Data Collection: Social media companies must be transparent about what data they collect and how they use it. They should also give users the option to opt-out of certain data collection practices.

5. Business Ethics: Social media companies must also adhere to ethical business practices, such as paying their taxes, avoiding exploitative labor practices, and treating their employees fairly.

6. Accessibility: Social media platforms should be accessible to everyone, regardless of their race, gender, ability, or economic status. The design of the platform should take into account the needs of all users.

7. Responsibility for Spread of Misinformation: Social media companies have a responsibility to combat the spread of misinformation on their platforms. They should ensure that their algorithms do not amplify false information, and they should work to promote accurate information.

8. Advertisements: Social media companies must ensure that advertisements on their platforms are not misleading or deceptive. They should also be transparent about who is paying for the ads and why they are being shown to users.

9. Addiction: Social media companies must also take into account the addictive nature of their platforms and take steps to minimize addiction, such as limiting the amount of time users spend on the site or providing tools for users to manage their usage.

10. Impact on Society: Social media companies must be aware of the impact their platforms have on society and take steps to minimize negative effects, such as the spread of

hate speech, division, and polarization.

Social media companies have a responsibility to ensure that their platforms are used ethically and responsibly. This requires a commitment to transparency, user privacy, and responsible business practices.

Corporate Social Responsibility And Social Media Companies

Corporate Social Responsibility (CSR) is the concept that businesses have a responsibility to consider the social, environmental, and economic impacts of their activities beyond just making profits. It involves taking a proactive approach to improving society and the environment, rather than just meeting legal requirements or minimizing harm.

Social media companies have a significant impact on society and the environment, making CSR an important consideration for them. For example, social media companies may undertake initiatives to reduce their carbon footprint, support local communities, or promote diversity and inclusion. Some social media companies have also made efforts to combat online harassment and hate speech, protect user data, and promote digital literacy.

The benefits of CSR for social media companies include increased brand reputation, customer loyalty, employee morale, and long-term profitability. Customers today increasingly expect companies to demonstrate a commitment to social responsibility, and companies that do so may be more likely to attract and retain customers. Employees are also more likely to feel engaged and motivated when working for a company with a strong sense of purpose and social impact.

However, there are also challenges and criticisms of CSR. Some argue that CSR initiatives may be ineffective or a form of "greenwashing" if they do not have a measurable impact on social or environmental issues. Additionally, some may argue that social responsibility conflicts with the pursuit of profit or that companies should focus on addressing social issues through charitable giving rather than changing their business practices.

To overcome these challenges, social media companies must consider the needs and perspectives of various stakeholders, including customers, employees, shareholders, and the wider community. This may involve setting clear goals and metrics for their CSR initiatives, involving stakeholders in decision-making, and communicating transparently about their efforts and impact.

Emerging trends in CSR for social media companies include the growing focus on sustainability and environmental responsibility, the rise of social impact investing, and the importance of ethical AI and data management. As social media continues to evolve and impact society, the role of CSR for these companies will become increasingly important in demonstrating a commitment to social and environmental responsibility.

Moreover, CSR goes beyond just making profits and involves considering the social, environmental, and economic impact of a company's activities. This means that social media companies have a responsibility to minimize any negative impacts their operations may have on society and the environment, while also maximizing their positive contributions.

Examples of CSR initiatives that social media companies have undertaken in the past include reducing their carbon footprint through the use of renewable energy and energy-efficient technologies, supporting local communities through charitable donations and volunteer work, promoting diversity and inclusion through hiring and training programs, and implementing strong data privacy and security measures to protect users' personal information.

The benefits of CSR for social media companies are numerous. By implementing CSR initiatives, companies can enhance their brand reputation, build customer loyalty, boost employee morale and retention, and increase their long-term profitability. In addition, CSR can help companies identify and mitigate potential risks to their business, such as legal and reputational issues.

However, there are also challenges and criticisms associated with CSR. One of the main challenges is measuring the impact of CSR initiatives, as it can be difficult to quantify the social and environmental benefits of these efforts. In addition, some critics argue that CSR can be used as a form of greenwashing, where companies use superficial or misleading CSR initiatives to distract from their negative impacts on society and the environment.

To address these challenges, social media companies must consider the needs and perspectives of various stakeholders in their CSR efforts, including customers, employees, shareholders, and the wider community. This means involving these groups in decision-making, setting clear goals and metrics, and communicating transparently about their efforts and impact.

Best practices for CSR in social media companies include conducting regular stakeholder engagement and impact assessments, setting ambitious sustainability targets, collaborating with other companies and organizations to address common challenges, and investing in ethical AI and data management practices.

Emerging trends in CSR for social media companies include a growing focus on sustainability and environmental responsibility, the rise of social impact investing, and the increasing importance of ethical AI and data management. By embracing these trends and implementing effective CSR strategies, social media companies can build a more sustainable and responsible future for themselves and society as a whole.

In addition to the benefits mentioned, CSR can also help social media companies to attract and retain talented employees, who are often motivated by a desire to work for companies that are making a positive impact in the world. CSR initiatives can also help to mitigate the risks of negative publicity or legal action resulting from unethical behavior or environmental damage.

However, there are also challenges and criticisms of CSR that social media companies need to be aware of. One challenge is the difficulty in measuring the impact of CSR initiatives, which can make it hard to assess their effectiveness and justify the investment. Another challenge is the potential for greenwashing, where companies make superficial or misleading claims about their environmental or social performance in order to enhance their reputation.

Critics of CSR argue that it can distract from the core business of making profits, and that companies should focus on maximizing shareholder value rather than pursuing social or environmental goals. There is also debate around the extent to which companies should be responsible for addressing social and environmental issues, and whether this is the role of governments and civil society organizations instead.

To address these challenges and criticisms, social media companies need to ensure that their CSR initiatives are well-designed, transparent, and aligned with their core business objectives. They also need to engage with stakeholders, including customers, employees, shareholders, and the wider community, to understand their needs and perspectives and involve them in decision-making. Finally, they need to stay up-to-date with emerging trends and best practices in CSR, and continually adapt their strategies and initiatives in response to changing social, environmental, and economic conditions.

The Ethical Considerations Of Data Collection And Monetization

Data collection and monetization raise ethical considerations for social media companies. These companies collect vast amounts of data about their users, often without explicit consent or knowledge, and use this data to generate revenue through targeted advertising and other means. This raises questions about the ethics of data collection, privacy, and transparency.

One ethical consideration is the issue of consent. Many users may not be aware of the extent to which their data is being collected and used, and may not have given explicit consent for this data to be collected and monetized. Social media companies have a responsibility to clearly communicate to users what data is being collected, how it will be used, and to obtain explicit consent for its use.

Another ethical consideration is the potential for misuse of data. Social media companies may use data to manipulate user behavior, such as by showing them ads or content that is designed to influence their opinions or actions. This raises concerns about the ethics of using personal data to manipulate user behavior without their knowledge or consent.

Social media companies also have an ethical responsibility to protect user data from misuse or unauthorized access. Data breaches and hacks can result in the theft of personal information, which can be used for identity theft and other malicious activities. Companies need to take appropriate measures to safeguard user data and be transparent about any breaches or vulnerabilities.

Finally, there is the issue of data monetization. Social media companies generate revenue through targeted advertising, which involves using user data to show ads that are more likely to be relevant to individual users. While this can be a useful and effective way to generate revenue, it raises questions about the ethics of monetizing personal data without the explicit consent of users.

Social media companies need to consider the ethical implications of data collection and monetization and take steps to ensure transparency, consent, and protection of user data.

The responsibility of social media companies in addressing social issues

Social media companies have become increasingly influential in shaping societal values and norms, and therefore they have a responsibility to address social issues. Social media platforms have the power to amplify marginalized voices and to facilitate conversations around social issues such as discrimination, inequality, and injustice.

One of the most pressing social issues facing society today is the spread of hate speech and misinformation on social media. Social media companies have a responsibility to monitor their platforms and take action against hate speech and other harmful content. This may involve implementing content moderation policies and algorithms, as well as providing resources and support for users who are targeted by hate speech or online harassment.

Another important social issue that social media companies can address is diversity and inclusion. Social media companies can promote diversity and inclusion by ensuring that their platforms are accessible to all users, regardless of their background or identity. This may involve implementing accessibility features, such as closed captioning for videos, as well as actively promoting diverse voices and perspectives on their platforms.

Social media companies also have a responsibility to address issues related to privacy and data protection. They must be transparent about their data collection and usage practices, and provide users with clear and easy-to-understand privacy policies. They should also take steps to protect user data from unauthorized access or misuse, and provide users with the ability to control and delete their data.

Finally, social media companies can play a role in addressing broader societal issues, such as climate change, by using their platforms to promote environmental awareness and sustainable practices. This may involve partnering with organizations that are working to address environmental issues, as well as promoting environmentally-friendly products and practices on their platforms.

In summary, social media companies have a responsibility to address social issues and to use their platforms to promote positive change in society. This requires a commitment to transparency, accountability, and ethical practices, as well as a willingness to engage with users and stakeholders on these important issues.

Chapter 8: What We Can Do About It

There are several things that individuals and society as a whole can do to address the negative impacts of social media. Some of which includes:

1. Educate ourselves: It is important to educate ourselves on the potential risks and negative impacts of social media use. This can include staying up to date on the latest research and news about social media and mental health, privacy concerns, and misinformation.

2. Practice responsible social media use: We can take steps to use social media in a responsible and healthy way, such as limiting our time on social media, setting boundaries around our social media use, and being mindful of the impact social media has on our mental health and well-being.

3. Advocate for change: We can advocate for change by putting pressure on social media companies to take responsibility for their impact on society and take steps to address issues such as privacy concerns, misinformation, and the spread of hate speech.

4. Support positive initiatives: We can support positive initiatives and campaigns that aim to promote responsible

social media use, combat misinformation, and address issues related to mental health and well-being.

5. Stay informed and engaged: We can stay informed and engaged on issues related to social media and its impact on society, and use our voices to call for change and hold social media companies accountable for their actions.

Here are some additional steps individuals can take to address the negative impacts of social media:

1. Practice self-regulation: Individuals can take responsibility for their own social media usage and set boundaries for themselves, such as limiting their screen time, taking breaks from social media, and avoiding engaging in toxic or divisive discussions.

2. Educate yourself and others: It's important to stay informed about the impact of social media on society and to share that knowledge with others. This can involve staying up-to-date on news and research related to social media and mental health, privacy concerns, and other social issues.

3. Advocate for change: Individuals can use their voices and platforms to advocate for changes in social media policies and practices. This can involve speaking out about the negative impacts of social media, supporting organizations that promote responsible social media use, and lobbying for government regulations that protect privacy and combat misinformation.

4. Support responsible social media companies: Individuals can choose to support social media companies that

prioritize ethical practices and social responsibility. This can involve using social media platforms that prioritize user privacy and safety, as well as supporting companies that have a track record of social and environmental responsibility.

5. Encourage healthy social media habits: Finally, individuals can encourage their friends, family, and communities to practice healthy social media habits, such as using social media in moderation, avoiding toxic conversations, and engaging in positive online communities.

How To Reduce The Negative Impact Of Social Media

There are several ways to reduce the negative impact of social media on individuals and society as a whole. Here are some suggestions:

1. Limit your social media use: One of the easiest ways to reduce the negative impact of social media is to limit your use. Try to set specific times each day for checking social media, and avoid using it excessively or late at night.

2. Be mindful of your social media consumption: When using social media, be mindful of what you are consuming. Try to avoid content that promotes negativity or has a negative impact on your mental health. Instead, focus on positive and uplifting content.

3. Educate yourself on privacy and security: Educate yourself on how social media companies collect and use your data,

and take steps to protect your privacy and security online. This can include adjusting your privacy settings, using two-factor authentication, and being cautious about sharing personal information online.

4. Support ethical social media companies: Support social media companies that prioritize ethical practices, such as transparency, data privacy, and social responsibility. Consider using social media platforms that prioritize user privacy and have a strong track record of ethical behavior.

5. Engage in positive online behavior: Finally, engage in positive online behavior by promoting kindness and empathy in your interactions on social media. Avoid cyberbullying, trolling, and hate speech, and instead promote respectful dialogue and constructive criticism.

Reducing the negative impact of social media requires a combination of individual responsibility and collective action. By being mindful of our social media use, supporting ethical companies, and promoting positive online behavior, we can help create a healthier and more positive online environment.

Tips For Responsible Social Media Use

Here are some tips for responsible social media use:

1. Set limits: Set a limit on the amount of time you spend on social media each day. This will help you avoid getting sucked into the endless scrolling and minimize the negative impact on your mental health.

2. Be mindful of your content: Before you post something

on social media, ask yourself if it adds value to your life or to the lives of others. Avoid posting anything that is hurtful, offensive, or promotes negativity.

3. Be aware of your privacy settings: Adjust your privacy settings to control who can see your content and personal information. Be cautious about what you share online, especially personal information such as your home address or phone number.

4. Practice critical thinking: Be aware that not everything you see on social media is true. Use critical thinking skills to evaluate information and sources before accepting them as fact.

5. Take breaks: Take regular breaks from social media to give your mind a rest and reduce the risk of addiction. Use that time to engage in other activities that benefit your mental and physical health, such as exercise or spending time with loved ones.

6. Be respectful: Treat others on social media with respect and kindness, even if you disagree with their opinions or beliefs. Avoid engaging in arguments or trolling behavior, and report any instances of cyberbullying or hate speech.

7. Seek support: If you are struggling with mental health issues related to social media use, seek support from a mental health professional or a support group. Remember that it is okay to take a step back and prioritize your mental health over social media.

Strategies For Creating A Healthier Relationship With Social Media

Here are some strategies for creating a healthier relationship with social media:

1. Set boundaries: Set limits on how much time you spend on social media each day. You can use apps that track your social media usage and set reminders to help you stay within your limits.

2. Engage mindfully: When using social media, be aware of your emotions and reactions. If you feel yourself getting overwhelmed, take a break or step away from social media for a while.

3. Follow positive accounts: Curate your social media feed to include accounts that inspire and motivate you. This can help counteract the negative impact of social media.

4. Be mindful of your self-talk: Be aware of the internal dialogue you have when using social media. Avoid comparing yourself to others and remember that social media is a curated version of reality.

5. Be selective with your sharing: Think carefully about what you share on social media and how it may impact others. Consider the potential consequences before posting anything that could be hurtful or offensive.

6. Practice digital detoxes: Take regular breaks from social media and give yourself time to disconnect and recharge.

7. Seek support: If you find yourself struggling with social media use, seek support from friends, family, or a mental health professional. They can help you develop healthy habits and coping strategies.

Here are some additional strategies for creating a healthier relationship with social media:

1. Set limits: Decide how much time you want to spend on social media each day and stick to it. Consider using a timer or setting specific times of day when you allow yourself to check social media.
2. Prioritize real-life relationships: Make an effort to connect with friends and family in person or through other forms of communication outside of social media. Engage in hobbies and activities that don't involve social media.
3. Be mindful of your content consumption: Pay attention to how the content you're consuming on social media makes you feel. If it's causing negative emotions or anxiety, consider unfollowing or muting accounts that don't contribute positively to your mental health.
4. Practice empathy and kindness online: Remember that there are real people behind the profiles on social media. Avoid engaging in negative or hurtful behavior and strive to create a positive online environment.
5. Take breaks: It's important to take regular breaks from social media to give your brain a rest and focus on other areas of your life. Consider taking a weekend or week-long break from social media to recharge and reset.

By implementing these strategies, you can create a healthier relationship with social media and reduce the negative impact it may have on your mental health and overall well-being.

Advocacy And Social Change Movements In Response To The Social Media Dilemma

As concerns around the negative impact of social media have grown, advocacy and social change movements have emerged in response. These movements aim to bring attention to the issue and promote changes in the way social media companies operate.

One such movement is the Time Well Spent movement, which was founded by Tristan Harris, a former Google employee who became concerned about the impact of technology on our attention and well-being. The movement advocates for the development of technology that is designed to prioritize human well-being, rather than just maximizing engagement and profits.

Another movement is the Center for Humane Technology, which was also founded by Tristan Harris and aims to change the design and business models of technology companies to better align with human values and well-being.

In addition to these movements, there have been various advocacy and social change efforts around specific issues related to social media, such as:

1. Cyberbullying: There have been many campaigns and initiatives aimed at raising awareness of cyberbullying and promoting strategies to prevent and address it.

2. Privacy and data protection: Advocacy groups have been pushing for stronger data protection laws and regulations, as well as educating the public on how to protect their privacy online.

3. Mental health: There have been numerous campaigns and

initiatives aimed at promoting mental health awareness and well-being, as well as advocating for changes in social media platforms that may contribute to mental health issues.

These movements and initiatives highlight the growing recognition of the need for responsible and ethical use of social media, and the importance of addressing the negative impacts it can have on individuals and society.

Chapter 9: Conclusion

In conclusion, social media has undoubtedly revolutionized the way we communicate, connect, and share information. It has brought many benefits, including increased access to information and opportunities for social and political engagement. However, it has also introduced new challenges, including the spread of misinformation, the erosion of privacy, and the negative impact on mental health.

As we have explored throughout this book, there are many ethical considerations to be made when it comes to social media. Social media companies have a responsibility to ensure the safety and well-being of their users, as well as to consider the broader social and environmental impact of their activities.

Fortunately, there are many steps that we can take as individuals, as well as collectively, to address these issues. By being responsible users of social media, we can reduce the negative impact it has on our mental health and personal privacy. By advocating for change and supporting social and environmental initiatives, we can encourage social media companies to prioritize the well-being of their users and the planet.

Furthermore, it is essential to recognize that the challenges posed by social media are not unique to this technology alone. They are part of a broader societal challenge to balance the benefits of technological progress with its potential risks and negative consequences. Therefore, it is critical that we continue to engage in critical dialogue and reflection on these issues to ensure that we are making informed and responsible choices about the role that social media plays in our lives.

In the future, we may see continued advancements in social media technology that bring new opportunities and challenges. It will be up to us as individuals and as a society to ensure that we are equipped to navigate these changes responsibly and ethically.

This book has aimed to provide a comprehensive overview of the social media dilemma, examining its impact on various aspects of society, its ethical considerations, and strategies for responsible use. It is our hope that it has inspired critical reflection and empowered readers to take action in creating a healthier relationship with social media.

Summary Of Key Points

Throughout this book, we have explored the complex and multifaceted impact of social media on our personal and societal well-being. We began by examining the ways in which social media can both facilitate and hinder our communication and social connections, highlighting the importance of responsible use and active engagement with our online communities.

We then delved into the various ways in which social media has reshaped our political landscape, from the rise of fake news and misinformation to the powerful influence of social media on election outcomes. We also explored the role of social media in shaping cultural norms and values, as well as the potential dangers of data collection and misuse.

Throughout these discussions, we emphasized the need for ethical considerations and corporate social responsibility in the development and implementation of social media platforms. We highlighted examples of CSR initiatives undertaken by social media companies, as well as the challenges and criticisms faced by such efforts.

We also provided practical tips and strategies for responsible social media use, including the importance of mindfulness, critical thinking, and digital detoxification. Finally, we discussed the role of advocacy and social change movements in response to the social media dilemma, emphasizing the importance of collective action and community building.

This book has illustrated the far-reaching impact of social media on our lives, both positive and negative. By examining the issues at hand and exploring potential solutions, we can work towards creating a healthier and more sustainable relationship with social media, one that promotes individual and societal well-being.

Final Thoughts On The Social Media Dilemma

The social media dilemma is a complex and multifaceted issue that requires careful consideration from all stakeholders. Social media has transformed the way we communicate, connect, and consume information, but it has also created a range of new challenges and risks that must be addressed.

Throughout this book, we have explored the various ways

that social media impacts our lives, from its influence on our mental health and personal privacy to its role in shaping political discourse and social movements. We have also examined the ethical considerations of data collection and monetization, as well as the responsibilities of social media companies in addressing social issues and promoting corporate social responsibility.

As we move forward, it is essential that we continue to have open and honest conversations about the impact of social media on our society. We must hold social media companies accountable for their actions and advocate for meaningful change that promotes the well-being of individuals and communities.

We also need to take personal responsibility for our own social media use and develop healthier relationships with these platforms. This includes being mindful of our online behavior, limiting our screen time, and prioritizing real-world connections over virtual ones.

While the social media dilemma is a complex and challenging issue, it also presents an opportunity for positive change. By working together, we can create a more responsible, equitable, and sustainable social media landscape that benefits everyone.

Call To Action For Readers To Take Control Of Their Social Media Use And Promote Positive Change

As we conclude our exploration of the social media dilemma, it is important to remember that we have the power to take control of our social media use and promote positive change. Social media has become an integral part of our lives, and it is unlikely to disappear anytime soon. Therefore, it is up to us to navigate the complexities of social media in a responsible and ethical manner.

To promote positive change, we must first acknowledge the negative impacts of social media, including its potential to contribute to mental health issues, political polarization, and the spread of misinformation. We can then take steps to reduce these negative impacts by implementing responsible social media use practices, such as limiting our time on social media, fact-checking information before sharing, and being mindful of the content we consume.

In addition to taking personal responsibility for our social media use, we can also advocate for change at the institutional level. This may include supporting regulatory efforts to hold social media companies accountable for their data collection and privacy practices, calling for greater transparency in algorithmic decision-making, and supporting efforts to combat online harassment and hate speech.

Ultimately, the social media dilemma is a complex issue that requires multifaceted solutions. By taking a proactive approach to our social media use and advocating for positive change, we can help create a more responsible and ethical social media landscape that serves the greater good.

Epilogue

Moving Forward with Social Media

As we come to the end of this book, it is clear that social media has revolutionized the way we connect, share information, and experience the world around us. However, it has also presented us with a range of challenges, from the spread of misinformation to issues of privacy and data collection.

It is clear that social media is here to stay, but it is up to us as individuals, as a society, and as the companies that create these platforms to determine how we want to interact with it. We have the power to create a healthier and more responsible relationship with social media, but it will require a collective effort and a commitment to change.

For individuals, this means taking responsibility for our social media use and making conscious decisions about how we engage with these platforms. This may involve setting boundaries, limiting our time on social media, and seeking out positive and informative content.

For society, it means creating a culture of digital literacy, where individuals are equipped with the knowledge and skills to navigate social media safely and responsibly. This may involve education programs in schools, public awareness campaigns, and initiatives to promote critical thinking and media literacy.

For the companies that create social media platforms, it

means recognizing their responsibility to promote ethical practices and to prioritize the well-being of their users over profit. This may involve implementing stronger privacy protections, increasing transparency about data collection and usage, and investing in initiatives that promote social responsibility and positive social change.

Ultimately, the social media dilemma is not a problem that can be solved overnight, but it is a challenge that we can meet if we work together. By taking control of our social media use and advocating for positive change, we can create a healthier and more responsible digital world for ourselves and for future generations.

Afterword

As we come to the end of this book, it is important to reflect on the insights we have gained about the social media dilemma. We have explored the many benefits and risks associated with social media, from its potential to connect people across the world to its ability to perpetuate harmful misinformation and contribute to negative mental health outcomes.

We have also examined the role of social media companies in collecting and monetizing user data, and the ethical considerations that come with this practice.

However, this book is not just about highlighting the problems of social media. It is also about empowering readers to take control of their own social media use and promoting positive change in the industry as a whole. We have discussed practical strategies for responsible social media use, as well as advocacy and social change movements that are working to address the issues at hand.

As we move forward, it is important to remember that social media is not inherently good or bad. It is a tool that can be used for positive or negative purposes, depending on how we choose to engage with it. By being mindful of our social media use, advocating for change, and promoting positive messages and content, we can help create a healthier digital world.

It is also important to recognize that the social media dilemma is not just an individual problem. It is a societal problem that requires collective action and systemic change. Social media companies have a responsibility to prioritize the well-being of their users and the wider community over their own profits.

Governments have a responsibility to regulate these companies and protect the privacy and rights of citizens. And we as individuals have a responsibility to hold these entities accountable and demand change.

In conclusion, the social media dilemma is complex and multifaceted, but it is not insurmountable. By working together and taking responsibility for our own actions, we can create a healthier, more positive digital landscape for ourselves and future generations.

Thank you for joining us on this journey, and we hope this book has inspired you to take action towards a better future.

www.ingramcontent.com/pod-product-compliance
Lightning Source LLC
La Vergne TN
LVHW051711050326
832903LV00032B/4141